THE
LUCKY STONE

Lucille Clifton

THE
LUCKY STONE

Illustrations by DALE PAYSON

Delacorte Press/New York

Published by
Delacorte Press
1 Dag Hammarskjold Plaza
New York, N.Y. 10017

Copyright © 1979 by Lucille Clifton
Illustrations copyright © 1979 by Dale Payson

Manufactured in the United States of America
Published simultaneously in Canada
First printing

Library of Congress Cataloging in Publication Data

Clifton, Lucille, 1936–
The lucky stone.
SUMMARY: A lucky stone provides good fortune for
its various owners.
I. Payson, Dale. II. Title.
PZ7.C6224Lu   [E]   78-72862
ISBN 0-440-05121-5
ISBN 0-440-05122-3 lib. bdg.

FOR WENDY THEN AND NOW

THE
LUCKY STONE

When I was a girl we lived all together in a house with a big wrap-around porch: me, my Mama and Daddy and my Great-grandmother, Mrs. Elzie F. Pickens. The F. stood for Free. She was about seventy some years old, my Great-grand. We used to sit out on that porch in good weather, and she would tell me stories about when she was a girl and the different things that used to happen and such as that.

Oh, I loved it so, I loved her so! Tee, she would call me. Sweet Baby Tee. Some of my favorite stories were her favorites too. Oh, how we both loved telling and hearing about the Lucky Stone!

ONE

On a hot June morning, Tee and her Great-grandmother were sitting on the porch in the sun. Tee had plumped the cushions in the rocker and helped her Great-grandmother get comfortable and park her stick. Then she sat on the first step right by the rocker and smiled.

"Tell me a story, Grandma."

And that smile was all Mrs. Pickens needed.

"That smile you got remind me of a lady," her Great-grandmother began, "remind me of a lady long long long time ago.

"This lady was named Vashti, and she lived with her Mama right down the road from me and mine. Her and her Mama used to sit out in the summertime on they front porch just rockin like this and smilin just like you, so pretty and polite.

"But we was all scared of them because they had real long fingernails on they fingers and long toenails on they toes. They never did say nothin to us or one another till one day me and my friends was passin by them soft-like.

"They was smilin and rockin on they porch, and the one Vashti leaned across the railin and whispered right to me, 'Girl, bring me glass a cool water I give you a lucky stone.'

"Now you know that scared me half to death but it wondered me too. And dog if I didn't light out and run back home and fetch back to that porch a long drink of cool water.

"Yes, and I can still hear them long
fingernails slickin on the glass while she
drank it all down her long throat.

"Then she made me come close to her
and she reached in her bosom and handed
me a warm stone, shiny black as nighttime
'cept for a scratch looked just like a letter A.
And she said the stone was mine. I tell you,
Sweet Tee, I was sayin my prayers I was so
scared, but I didn't let on.

" 'Thank you, ma'am, but that's all right,' I said to her. But she come right close with her face to the porch rail. 'Take it. I got no other chick nor chile. It's a lucky stone,' she said. So I took it and kept it and got it still and one fine day I'm gonna give it to you, Sweet Tee.

"And the story of that stone is this.

"When Vashti's Mama, Miss Mandy, was a little girl it was slavery time. One day when she was workin in the hot sun pickin cotton, a mean old snake come creepin up on her by her foot and she gave a holler and fell down and dumped the sack she was carryin. It split wide open and all the cotton was ruined, don't you know, a whole load of cotton!

"Now she was just a girl but she was scared 'cause she was due for a beatin indeed, and she didn't want to be whipped by that mean old bossman. She hadn't never been whipped before, and she had promised herself she never would be. So she just started creepin easy and fast and low down in the field so nobody could see her.

"But the bossman saw her anyhow and started toward her on his horse with the whip in his hand. And she lit out so scared and ran off from the field and hid in a cave.

"Come dark she was too scared to go back and come day again she was too scared 'cause she had been gone all night. One day become two and two days become three and on the third day she heard dogs far off and knew she couldn't go back or move from where she was. That little girl.

"Well, didn't nobody know where she was, slave nor free, when one evening after near a week had gone by, an old driver from the plantation was ridin by that cave bringin the carriage when a stone shot out and spooked his horse. That horse reared up but the driver held him and got him stopped and steady and then he got down to see what it was had hit his horse. And he found on the ground a stone black as night.

"Well, that old man was disgusted that one little stone was makin him lose time like that. So he picked it up and threw it back into the cave.

"And Tee, do you know that while he was walkin back to the carriage that stone come sailin out of the cave again and hit him on the neck! That old driver grabbed it up where it fell and looked at it and knew it for the same stone, black as night. But this time it had the letter *A* scratched on one side. Now Miss Mandy's right name was Amanda, you know, and her old Mizz had showed her the letters of it one time. So of course now everybody slave knew where the child was hid.

"After that every week regular some slave would walk or ride by the way of that cave and lose somethin there, sometime a chicken and sometime some fruit and sometime some potatoes and homemade bread. Every natural week until emancipation. Weeks and months, Tee Baby, more than a year.

"After emancipation the girl came out from that cave with wild hair and eyes and with them long fingernails on her fingers and long toenails on her toes. And she had that stone with her and she give it to her daughter, Vashti, when she got one. And like I have told you, Vashti give it to me."

The sun was almost gone. Tee stretched and yawned and went to help her Great-grandmother up from the rocker and to hand her her stick.

"Grandma, why was the stone lucky?"

"Well, if she hadn't heard that old horse and hit him and that old man with it so folks would know where she was, she would most likely have starved to death, Sweet Tee. That's how it was lucky for her and it was lucky for Vashti too. And someday I might tell you about that." She smiled.

And they both went in for lemonade.

TWO

Mrs. Elzie F. Pickens and her Great-granddaughter Tee were singing "Jesus Keep Me Near the Cross" toward evening on the porch.

Her Great-grandmother smiled when the song was over.

"Your voice is so sweet, my Tee, it reminds me of my own mother singin."

"Was she a real singer, Great-grand?" Tee asked.

"Oh, she used to be the lead singer in the Greater Glory Baptist Church Choir, Baby. They had meeting every Sunday, and they used to sing that song. She sang the lead from the time when she was a young girl.

"And now that puts me in the mind of something I said I would tell you one time."

"What, Grandma?" Tee settled back against the porch railing.

And that was the beginning of that story.

"That puts me in mind of the time my Mama told me about," said Mrs. Pickens.

"After emancipation, when the colored people were free to travel and move around more, they could learn how to read and write and most everybody was anxious to do it. They could have church all out in the open then, too, so they started a church. And a choir.

"My Mama was just a young girl then
but she sang the lead right off. They had
something like a stage built out in the field
under the trees, you know. They would
gather there and have singin and preachin
and a good time. The Reverend Matthew
James Jones was the circuit preacher and
they tell me he was a mighty man of God.

"Now you remember 'bout Miss Mandy and her daughter, Vashti? Well, Vashti was just a girl then herself, not yet so long-nailed and folks weren't so scared of her as they were of her Mama, Miss Mandy.

"Anyhow, this time I'm talking about, a meetin was to be held on Sunday afternoon. Everybody was eager to be there. It was a strange threatenin day like we have sometime in late summer. Thunder soundin from somewhere off and lightnin seem like it's just about to come.

"I tell you, Sweet Tee, ain't nothin quite as heavy on you as a storm that seem to be headin your way. Everybody decided to attend the meeting though, because Reverend Jones didn't get around but every so often.

"I just know it seemed beautiful under the trees, everybody sittin on the grass around the stage wearin their pretty meetin shawls and smilin and howdyin each and all.

"Under those trees I 'magine the sky didn't seem so heavy. They tell me that the Greater Glory Baptist Church Choir gathered there on the stage and sang three or four numbers endin up with my own mother singin the lead on 'Jesus Keep Me Near the Cross.' There was shoutin and happiness and people grown and small rushin forward to testify.

"They tell me a man named Kenford Gamble run up and confessed every one of his sins, and it took him a good forty minutes with the thunder threatenin and the saints all full of amen.

"It was a time, a time!

"Then they tell me some young people walked up on that stage one by one and stood there alone.

"Vashti was the last. She just stood there movin back and forth and back and forth, and all of a sudden she reached her arms out and flung 'em wide and started singin 'Jesus Keep Me Near the Cross.' She was wearin a string 'round her neck, and on the string was a pouch. Don't you know while she was singin the string broke and the pouch fell off her, and it bounce one time and then bounce again off the stage.

"Vashti stopped right in the middle of singin. She put her arms down and stood still for a minute. The people all got still. Even the skies seemed to stop their threatenin and be still. Vashti stood there on the stage by herself.

"Then she said all of a sudden, 'My stone!' and she jumped right down to the ground from the stage and reached for the pouch. And bless Jesus, just as she jumped down the storm broke! A great arm of God's lightnin shot out of the sky and struck that stage right where Vashti had been standin!

"Oh, everybody jumped up and started scramblin and runnin for home, but not 'fore they saw the stage catch fire and crumble to the ground.

"Vashti picked up her pouch, they say, and poured out this stone, shiny and black as night, and just held it in her hand."

They sat for a while in the twilight.

"That stone was sure lucky for her, Grandmama," Tee whispered after a while.

"That's 'cause it's a lucky stone." Her Great-grandmother smiled.

"Was it ever lucky for you, Grandmama?"

Mrs. Pickens chuckled.

"Well, I just might tell you about that some day, Baby."

And they went into the house.

THREE

Mrs. Elzie F. Pickens was rocking slowly on the porch one afternoon when her Great-granddaughter brought her a big bunch of dogwood blooms, and that was the beginning of that story.

"Ahhh, now that dogwood reminds me of the day I met your Great-granddaddy, Mr. Pickens, Sweet Tee.

"It was just this time, spring of the year, and me and my best friend Ovella Wilson, who is now gone, was goin to join the Silas Greene. Usta be a kinda show went all through the South, called it the Silas Greene show. Somethin like the circus. Me and Ovella wanted to join that thing and see the world. Nothin wrong at home or nothin, we just wanted to travel and see new things and have high times. Didn't say nothin to nobody but one another. Just up and decided to do it.

"Well, this day we plaited our hair and put a dress and some things in a crokasack and started out to the show. Spring day like this.

"We got there after a good little walk and it was the world, Baby, such music and wonders as we never had seen! They had everything there, or seemed like it.

"Me and Ovella thought we'd walk around for a while and see the show before goin to the office to sign up and join.

"While we was viewin it all we come up on this dancin dog. Cutest one thing in the world next to you, Sweet Tee, dippin and movin and head bowin to that music. Had a little ruffly skirt on itself and up on two back legs twistin and movin to the music. Dancin dancin dancin till people started throwin pennies out of they pockets.

"Me and Ovella was caught up too and laughin so. She took a penny out of her pocket and threw it to the ground where that dog was dancin, and I took two pennies and threw 'em both.

"The music was faster and faster and that dog was turnin and turnin. Ovella reached in her sack and threw out a little pin she had won from never being late at Sunday school. And me, laughin and all excited, reached in my bag and threw out my lucky stone!

"Well, I knew right off what I had done. Soon as it left my hand it seemed like I reached back out for it to take it back. But the stone was gone from my hand and Lord, it hit that dancin dog right on his nose!

"Well, he lit out after me, poor thing. He lit out after me and I flew! Round and round the Silas Greene we run, through every place me and Ovella had walked before, but now that dancin dog was a runnin dog and all the people was laughin at the new show, which was us!

"I felt myself slowin down after a while and I thought I would turn around a little bit to see how much gain that cute little dog was makin on me. When I did I got such a surprise! Right behind me was the dancin dog and right behind him was the finest fast runnin hero in the bottoms of Virginia.

"And that was Mr. Pickens when he was still a boy! He had a length of twine in his hand and he was twirlin it around in the air just like the cowboy at the Silas Greene and grinnin fit to bust.

"While I was watchin how the sun shined on him and made him look like an angel come to help a poor sinner girl, why, he twirled that twine one extra fancy twirl and looped it right around one hind leg of that dancin dog and brought him low.

"I stopped then and walked slow and shy to where he had picked up that poor dog to see if he was hurt, cradlin him and talkin to him soft and sweet. That showed me how kind and gentle he was, and when we walked back to the dancin dog's place in the show he let the dog loose and helped me to find my stone. I told him how shiny black it was and how it had the letter *A* scratched on one side. We searched and searched and at last he spied it!

"Ovella and me lost heart for shows then and we walked on home. And a good little way, the one who was gonna be your Great-granddaddy was walkin on behind. Seein us safe. Us walkin kind of slow. Him seein us safe. Yes." Mrs. Pickens' voice trailed off softly and Tee noticed she had a little smile on her face.

"Grandmama, that stone almost got you bit by a dog that time. It wasn't so lucky that time, was it?"

Tee's Great-grandmother shook her head and laughed out loud.

"That was the luckiest time of all, Tee Baby. It got me acquainted with Mr. Amos Pickens, and if that ain't luck, what could it be! Yes, it was luckier for me than for anybody, I think. Least mostly I think it."

Tee laughed with her Great-grandmother though she didn't exactly know why.

"I hope I have that kind of good stone luck one day," she said.

"Maybe you will someday," her Great-grandmother said.

And they rocked a little longer and smiled together.

I have my Great-grandmother Mrs. Elzie F. Pickens' lucky stone now, but she never handed it to me.

And here is the story of that.

FOUR

Up until the time I was fourteen years old I hadn't ever got one valentine in the mail. And I was really worried about having a boyfriend and all. I used to talk to my Great-grandmother about it.

"Don't you worry, Sweet Tee." She would smile and pat my plaits. "They'll come round buzzin like bees to the cone, bees to the cone."

The year that I was going to be fourteen was the year that she was almost eighty years old and caught pneumonia. Oh, that scared us. She was such an old woman. Real little and thin, but not weak-looking, just a small old lady. She would lay in her bed watching the sun out the window and breathing so loud seemed like her breathing rustled the curtains.

After a few days Mama and Daddy wanted to take her to the hospital, but she didn't want to go.

"I'll let the sun heal me," she'd fuss. "Give the sun just one more good day."

"Grandmother, you need the doctor," Mama would almost cry.

"The sun be my doctor if it's all right with you," my Great-grandmother would say.

But finally Mama and Daddy took her to the hospital. And every day without missing I would walk to the hospital with dogwood or candy and every day the nurse wouldn't let me see my Great-grandmother.

"No visitors." That's all she would say.
No reason or nothing. No visitors.

Well, this one day I went over to the hospital and the nurse's place was empty. I didn't even think about it; soon as I saw nobody was there I went looking for my Great-grandmother. Found her too. She was in the fourth room I tried, a little tiny old lady in a big old bed. Not enough sun or nothing. I was in the room before she saw me.

"Ohhh, it's my Baby, my Sweet Tee Baby." She laughed. She was so glad to see me.

And I ran to the bed and hugged her hard because I was so glad to see her too. And I started to cry.

"Why what is the matter, Tee?"

"Oh, Grandma." I was talkin and cryin at the same time. "Grandmama, I ain't never gonna have no boyfriend and nobody will ever love me but you, and I couldn't even get in here to see you and I ain't gonna never have nobody."

My Great-grand hugged me hard.

"Hush your mouth, girl," she laughed, "hush up now. You talk like you ain't kin to me. You'll have the ones you want and the ones you don't. Sweet Tee, they be on you like bees to the cone. And you ain't done with me neither, not yet." And she seemed to be laughing more.

Well, that old nurse came in just then and made me go.

"When you get home, look on my dresser. Don't forget. Look on my dresser," my Great-grandmother called to me on my way out.

That evening after my Mama and Daddy went out to the hospital I went into my Great-grand's room and sat in her chair. Her room smelled old and warm and sweet like she did.

I went over to her dresser like she told
me. I looked at the pictures all framed in
lace and gold. There were aunts and un-
cles I didn't know. And Mama when she
was a little girl and Mama's Mama, my
Grandmother and my Great-grand's own
daughter who was gone before I was born.

And right by the picture of Mama's
Mama was a lace hanky with an envelope
half folded in it. And the envelope had my
name on it! Tee!

I unfolded the hanky and took the envelope over to the rocker and sat down and
opened it up.   There was something inside
warm and black as night, a stone with a
letter scratched on one side like an *A*.   The
stone!

Oh, I held it and kissed it and rocked and cried in that chair and that was where they found me when they came in that evening. My Mama and my Daddy and my Great-grandmother well again!

They laughed when they saw me sitting curled up asleep in my Great-grand's chair with the lucky stone clutched in my hand. They say they did anyway.

Next day I got in the mail my very first valentine, a big red heart edged in lace, and my Great-grandmother laughed and called me Honeycone, and it seemed like I smiled all day. It was the prettiest thing I had ever seen and it was signed just J.D., and I didn't even know that anybody called by that was looking at me when I watched him in school so much.

The world is a wondrous place.

Now that is the story of how I got my lucky stone and how it started being lucky for me. There is more to it than that though, and someday I might tell you about that too.

About the Author

LUCILLE CLIFTON is an award-winning poet and the author of many notable children's books, including the popular Everett Anderson books and *The Times They Used to Be,* available in a Dell Yearling edition. She lives in Baltimore, Maryland, with her husband and their six children.

About the Artist

DALE PAYSON is a free-lance illustrator. She grew up in White Plains, New York, and studied art at the School of Visual Arts. She has illustrated many children's books and lives in New York City.

About the Book

The illustrations for this book were drawn with a pencil on bond vellum. The text was set in Aster by Arrow Typographers, Inc. The book was printed by The Maple-Vail Book Manufacturing Group and bound by Economy Bookbinding Corp. Designed by Lynn Braswell.